THORNTON IN TIMES PAST
Alan Whitworth

Text © Alan Whitworth, 1987, 2003
Published by Culva House Publications Printed by Jetprint, Whitby.
ISBN 1 871150 25 6

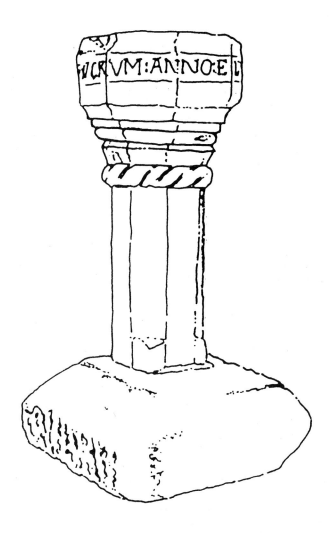

Inscribed and dated 'Aqua Perficit Adla Vacrum : Anno : D 1679' – which loosely translated means 'All Who Pass Through These Waters are Made Perfect', four of the Bronte children were baptised in this font from the old Bell Chapel, which is now in the Church of St James, Thornton. Drawn by Alan Whitworth.

INTRODUCTION

To many, particularly devotees of the Bronte's, the name Thornton will be well-known, as it was here, in the year 1815, as the Duke of Wellington was defeating Napoleon at Waterloo, and in consequence, turning the war with France toward a peace, that the Rev. Patrick Bronte took up his clerical duties with a wife and two young children. Five years later he moved to a final incumbency at Haworth — yet in that brief period at Thornton, with the birth of Charlotte, Branwell, Emily and Anne, the foundation of a literary phenomenan was laid which has in this century, brought fame to the area — but the story of Thornton does not just begin at this point.

The origins of the village go back before the Norman 'Conquest', when Thornton belonged to the manor of Bolton. It is spelt in the Domesday Book as 'Torenton' meaning 'enclosure of Thorns', but it is possible that the district had been settled prior to the ninth century as a number of funeral urns have been excavated over the years at Thornton and in the immediate vicinity, thus evidence is not wanting that for instance, the picturesque mound upon which Headley is situate, was inhabited at a very early period of British history by those warriors who painted themselves blue with woad.

According to John James, a noted local historian, as early as 1150 a family by the name of Thornton held large possessions here, and as a consequence obtained the privileges of a manor, the first notable lord being Hugh de Thornton. The Bollings of Bolling Hall were descendants of the Thorntons, and after them the manor passed by marriage to Sir Richard Tempest of Bracewell (Lancs) until, in 1620, it was sold. About 1638 the manor was sold yet again, returning to local ownership by being bought by the Midgleys, and through them it was retained until 1715, when it was conveyed by Josiah Midgley along with the Headley estate and Hall where he resided, to John Cockcroft, Attorney of Bradford.

It was while Thornton was in the possession of the Tempest family, that a medieval deer park was formed. The park, of which we have a survival in the name Doe park, now a reservoir from which Bradford derives part of its water supply, encompassed several miles and was well stocked with red deer for hunting. It consisted of the high park and the low (Doe) park. It is thought that Denholme Gate as it is now named, formed the main entrance. Another principal entrance remains, Thorn-gate, and there was another gate probably at Cullingworth. A considerable part of the park wall existed well into this century. In 1746, a moiety (half share) of the manor, including Headley, was purchased by a John Stanhope, and another moiety by the Horton family, from whom it descended with the manor of Horton to one Captain Rhyss, on his marriage to the daughter of Sir Watts Horton. From him, the manor went to W.S. Stanhope, Esq. and Lady Stocks. Following the Enclosure Acts, and the enclosing of the moors and wastelands of Thornton in 1771, the manor was effectively dispersed.

The amount and type of land enclosed under the aforementioned Acts, over 900 acres of moor alone, gives a certain substance to the many writers comments that Thornton was a 'wild, bleak and desolate' spot up until the early 19th century — and an entry in the Bradford parish church registers dated 23rd December 1630, reading 'a poor stranger found dead on ye moor in Thornton' reveals how treacherous the terrain could really be.

Little is recorded about Thornton during the 16th and 17th centuries. Hardly surprising however, as it was at that time an insignificant township, and even though Bradford came under seige during the Civil War, districts such as Thornton were totally ignored by such historic events. Even as late as 1800, there were still only 23 dwellings forming the village itself, and three of these were public houses! The centre of these houses lay around what is known today as Market Street, which was then the main road from Bradford to Halifax and beyond, but there were little clusters of buildings — hamlets — at School Green, West Scholes, Close Head, Kipping, Headley and Leventhorpe, of which concerning the latter two, fine substantial halls were built during the 16th century.

Undoubtedly, the village today presents an aspect of 19th century enterprise. No 'great' religious house took interest in the land during the Middle Ages, possibly because it was unsuitable for arable farming and too inaccessible for grazing, so it was not until the mid-1800s, when 'expansion' was the word on every enterpreneurs lips, that Thornton saw development. The National School on the north side of the Market Street was built in 1831. The present St. James's church was built in 1872 to replace an older edifice. Thornton Mechanics Institute was conceived in 1835; a building was constructed in 1870. The Local Board was first elected in 1865. Gas was supplied into the area by the Clayton, Allerton and Thornton Gas Company and the Thornton branch of the Bradford, Halifax and Keighley Railway was started with the first sod being cut on March 11th, 1874 and opened as far as the village, in 1878. This led later, to the erection of one of the most outstanding features of the Pinch Beck Valley at Alderscholes, the 120 foot high, twenty arch railway viaduct.

It was at this time too, that the textile trade, with its roots in the previous centuries, was consolidated, and between 1826-1870 a number of mills were built in and around Thornton, notably Upper Mill, which occupied the site where Downs Coulters now stands, and Dole and Prospect Mills. The stone trade was also an important element of the district. Of great repute for general building purposes and found in large quantities about the area, the original sandstone quarries were only small, and known locally as 'delfs', but large commercial quarrying was established in the early 19th century and tiny communities sprang up as a result at Moscow and later Egypt. In the 1870s, throughout the Local Board district of Thornton, 30 quarries were recorded. There were several colleries too, and alongside this seam of coal ran a good band of fire clay, and during the time 1870 to 1880 a fireclay trade of some size was established at Thornton.

Yet for all that, despite incorporation with Bradford in 1899 and steady growth since, Thornton has managed to retain to itself an air of remoteness — and is still in principle, a village community, self-sufficient and almost scornful of the 20th century City of Bradford on its doorstep.

Acknowledgements

I should like to acknowledge the following people for their generous permission to reproduce illustrations: Lilywhite Postcards of Brighouse 11, 13, 21, 29; Bradford Telegraph & Argus 18, 45; Commercial Graphic Co. 19; C. H. Wood Ltd 25; Dorothy Burrows 26, 33; Real Photographic Co. 46; Alan Whitaker Collection 46; Yorkshire Life 47. Also to the many others who have made contributions to this work, in particular the late Arthur Saul, of Hill Top, former Conservation Officer, Bradford MC. Lastly, I should like to mention the two who inspired this book, my darling children John and Susi Whitworth, the last of whom has grown-up beyond my greatest expectations.

Many writers of the 19th century commented on the 'wild and remote' aspect of Thornton, and even today, as in the 1950s when the photograph of a windy Market Street on the title page was taken, little has changed in this respect.

In the *Domesday Book* Thornton is spelt 'Torenton' meaning 'enclosure among the thorns' – possibly taking its name from the generally treeless character of the neighbourhood which would have given prominence to even the stunted Hawthorns whose 'milk-white blossoms' often 'scent the evening gale'. Journal of Bradford Antiquarian Society, 1888.

As seen here, the old chapel of St. James, whose ruins stand in the redundant graveyard across from the present parish church of Thornton, represents the tireless zeal and enterprise of the Rev. Patrick Bronte, father of those literary figures, Charlotte, Ann and Emily Bronte — and following restoration, a dated wooden board on the exterior bore witness to this fact; it read 'This Chapel was Repaired and Beautified 1818. P. Bronte, incumbent'. His 'repairs' entailed the demolition and rebuilding of the south wall with the insertion of spacious windows, the complete re-roofing of the church, and the erection of the cupola and re-instatement of the 'old' bell — both of which gave the edifice later, the local name of 't'owd bell chapel'. It is interesting to note that the tower was undoubtably built first or in existence, and the cupola was brought from elsewhere and added on — as it clearly does not fit!

In 1888, Erskine Stuart described the 'Bell Chapel' as 'mean-looking... with an unambitious cupola. It is in the Gothic style, but so bare and unpretentious, as to appear like an old dissenting meeting-house'. True, it is perhaps oddly proportioned, but it hardly merits so vindictive a description. Today, of this building, in which the Bronte family worshipped, a few artefacts can be seen in the new church; a holy water-stoup of 1687, inscribed with the names of the churchwardens, an old chest dated 1685, and a font carrying the Latin inscription 'Aqua Perficit Adla Vacrum AD 1679' which implies 'Through Water All are Made Free' — in which, all of the Bronte children were baptised. Recently, a considerable amount of stonework from the dismantled edifice was rediscovered built into a garden wall in the grounds of adjoining Thornton Hall Farm, in the ownership of Mr. & Mrs. A. Brown, including early and sculptured pieces, and a curious hexagonal window with mason's marks, that cannot be seen in old illustrations.

Prior to alteration 'inside the building it was damp, dark and extremely dismal; two galleries all but blocked out the light emitted by the small square windows. . . having no organ, the singers and fiddlers performed from the east gallery. Fearing its structure unsound, Patrick had them brought down'. In 1755, new pews were set up and a seating plan drawn (below). The list contains such names as Sir William Horton for Thornton Hall (1); Dr. Hill for Low Mill (14); Denholme House and Squire York lands (22); Dean House (10); Jonas Pearson for Hoyle Ing (6); Mr. Hollins for Cote Gap (13); and Ye Revd. Wm. Lamplugh, clerk (8).

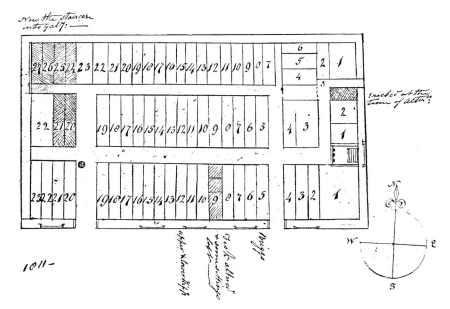

In June 1815 Patrick Bronte moved himself, his young wife and two babies — Maria and Elizabeth — from Hartshead to this house, 74 Market Street, Thornton. Built in 1802 by John and Sarah Asworth, who were responsible for the erection of Clogger's Row, it stood at that time detached from other dwellings overlooking sloping fields.

Born of a poor Irish family, on Sunday, August 10th 1806, Patrick Bronte was ordained Deacon in Fulham Palace Chapel, and by October of the same year he was established in his first curacy, Wethersfield, Essex. He was ordained into the priesthood on Monday, December 21st 1807, in the Chapel Royal of St. James, Westminster.

Following the Bronte's departure to Haworth, a second vicarage was built, and the 'Parsonage' with the addition of a shopfront became a butchers — and livestock were slaughtered in a small abattoir at the back. In Patrick Bronte's day there was a 'dining room on one side of the hall, and a drawing room on the other'. The window above the doorway, lit a dressing room. 'It was at Haworth that Mr.

Bronte's gifted children. . . achieved literary fame. . . but their birth-place was here. . . a fact of which the inhabitants of that village ought to feel proud. But until the spot. . . is rescued from the "base uses" to which it is now put, and restored to something of its original semblance and dignity, any attempt to honour their memory. . . must be regarded as incomplete'. — Wm. Scruton, 1898.

Now a DoE Grade II listed monument after a vigorous campaign by the Society for the Promotion of the Preservation of English Parish Churches, the ruins display a number of early date stones and a carved inscription which reads, 'This Chappell was Builded by ------IIII-E, Freemason in the Yeare of Our Lorde 1612' — however, there is little doubt after extensive research that that original foundation may be of 13th century date, and that the ruins stand on a site possibly occupied by three separate consecutive churches. There is a reference to a 'Robert the Clerk del Sarte' as a witness to a Leventhorp deed and it is probable that the first edifice was a chantry chapel-of-ease associated with an early Thornton Hall. Such chapels were often erected and endowed by lords of the manor as they were exempt from ecclesiastical dues, and in West Yorkshire they were a common occurence in the ecclesiastical system but often escaped official recognition because of the previous statement.

Of the possible three churches which stood on this site, the first would be a simple two- or three-celled building, then later, as the population and status of Thornton grew, another would be erected at which point most, if not all of the original chapel was swept away — certainly little was preserved in the fabric of the second church if indeed anything, and nothing has survived the third rebuild of the 17th century. Of the second chapel which probably followed the ground plan of the original, there remains the impressive east window of the ruins with the donors heads charmingly displayed. This window is almost identical with one at Headley Hall. Further than the east window, little is left of the early churches at Thornton, but historically, it was probably during the existence of this building that the dedication was changed to St. James from St. Leonard as recorded in a document dated 1560.

The site for the new church, half an acre, was given by John Foster, of Queensbury and Hornby Castle; designs for the church were drawn by the architects, T.H. & F. Healey, and on the 26th of October, 1870, the foundation stone was laid by the Rigt Hon. Early de Grey and Ripon, K.G. in grand Masonic style. The mallet used on the occasion was that used at the laying of the foundation stone of St. Paul's Cathedral. The new church, which is solidly built in the Early English style of architecture, is a striking object in the dale which it overlooks. 'It would be a picturesque one, too, if only a few clusters of trees could be grown in proximity to it.'

Cloggers' Row, Market Street put up in 1806 during the reign of King George IV, between the battles of Trafalgar and Waterloo. Here can be found on one of the workmen's cottages, the date and initials showing that they were built for John and Sarah Ashworth who owned many properties in the village including the Parsonage House, home of the Bronte's, which also bears the initials JAS and the date 1802.

The origin of the old Independant Congregation at Kipping cannot be fixed with certainty. There is a tradition that the Kipping 'Congregation' first met openly at Well Heads, above Thornton, in the days of the 'Long Parliament', called together by Charles I in 1640 — however, it may date back to the days of Queen Elizabeth I, but it is recorded that following the 'Act of Uniformity' in 1662, compelling everyone to conform to the rites of the Church of England, until 1672, the Independant Congregation met illegally, mostly in a barn down Lower Kipping Lane. Kipping Congregational Chapel at the south side of Market Street, was built on its present site in 1769, it was enlarged in 1807 and again in 1823, and was largely rebuilt in 1843.

The Mechanics' Institute was established in 1834 with the object of the 'dissemination of useful knowledge and the social intercourse and recreation of its members'. First conducted in rented accommodation the foundation stone of a purpose-built property was laid on 2 July 1870 by Mr Joseph Craven.

A popular aspect of the Institutes social life was the Operatic and Dramatic Society, and in October 1922 a production of Gilbert & Sullivan's comic opera *The Gondoliers* was staged. The principals in the production included Mr A. Craven, as the Duke; Mr S. Robinson, as Luiz, his attendant; Miss M. Spencer, as the Duchess; Mr & Mrs A. Clarke; Mrs Herbert Pickles; Master G. Crossland, as the Drummer Boy; and Master L. Robinson as the Page Boy. The Musical Director was Mr J. W. Horsfall and the accompanist was Mrs M. Robinson. Photographs, including the above, were taken by Jack Ronald.

In 1894, a recreation ground was constructed at Hill Top, and opened to the public in March of that year. The cost of laying it out and constructing a boundary wall, entrances, etc amounted to £1,482. In area it contained over four acres. Here football was played, and undoubtedly the team above, winners of the 1913-1914 Championship, held sway. By 1931 portions of land adjoining the Allotment Gardens, containing an area of over two acres, were laid out as a Bowling Green and three hard tennis courts, and a children's playing area was also provided on land at Royd Street, acquired for this purpose from the Water Committee.

1898. Class F Thornton St. James's National School — Master: William Williams. Mistress: Mrs. Phoebe Williams. 'Writing on the whole, is pretty fair, but it would be greatly improved, I am convinced, were more attention paid in Standards I and II to the accurate formation and proportion of the letters, and were Standard III as well as the upper Standards encouraged to write more on paper. Often I find traces in Standard IV of an inability to write with freedom. . . . (on paper) . . . where Standard III has written accurately, and with rapidity on their slates. Writing on paper is after all the only way in which it will hereafter be useful; for who ever uses a slate out of school?' — School Inspectors Report (Church of England Schools).

From the second half of the 18th century there are a few surviving examples of squatters' cottages erected on common and wasteland. The men who built these dwellings were occasionally mentioned in manorial court records. One such entry, dated 1775, records that Ake Akroyd enclosed half an acre of land in Thornton. The cottage above, in Half Acre Lane, is likely to have superseded and earlier, less substantial, squatters' cottage. Other similar cottages sited haphazardly on roadsides and commons are found in mining and quarrying areas and are likely to have been built on land similarly encroached upon. In time clusters of these properties became communities and around Thornton acquired improbable names such as Egypt, World's End, Moscow, and Paris – all found within a half mile radius of each other.

The original site of Thornton Grammar School was at School Green, on land bought in 1672. Four local benefactors liberally gave lands and tenements in and around Bradford, the rents from which allowed the building of a small classroom that was opened in 1673. The stone entrance from this (left) was removed to the new school, and bears the inscription 'Gymnasium Literarium Sculti Doctrinam Spernunt 1673'. The school at School Green is clearly marked on an Enclosure Map of Thornton dated 1771 and remained in use until 1874. The first definitely recorded headmaster, was the Rev. James Ward (1690-1702).

In 1876 a new Thornton Grammar School was erected on land adjoining Thornton Baths, obtained from Joseph Craven, of Ashfield, Thornton. The architects for the school were T.H & F. Healey, of Bradford, and it cost in total £2,600 including furnishings!

The first headmaster of this complex was the Rev. T. Waldron, who wrote in his first Annual Report, 'I opened the school on the 15th January 1877 with 27 pupils, subsequently increasing to 31. My first few days were spent in examining the character and extent of the attainments of my new pupils. I was pleased with the healthy freshness of tone exhibited generally by the boys, though I found myself unable altogether to acquiesce in the excellent opinion which some of the more advanced ones appeared to entertain of their attainments!'

Well Heads Congregational School built AD 1859, is inscribed above the door. The abundance of water and water courses which were fed from the hills round about provided a number of placenames and the district abounds with such titles as 'Manywells', 'Well Heads', and 'Spring Holes'. Denholme is a compound of the word 'dene' and 'holm', the former meaning valley in Saxon and the latter signifying 'land enclosed by water'. In 1770 during the reign of King George III, an Act of Parliament was obtained for inclosing the moor and waste lands of the manor of Thornton. The result was that about 900 acres about Well Head, skirting Denholme Park, Thornton Heights, Foreside, and up to Oxenhope were 'walled in' during the following year, giving us today the landscape that is familiar to the inhabitants.

Not until the 19th century was Thornton's landscape finally tamed. Prior to the Enclosure Acts, the majority of land hereabouts was rugged moor and even in the mid-19th century, Mrs. Gaskell among many, thought 'the neighbourhood desolate and wild; great tracts of bleak lands enclosed by stone dykes, sweeping upward...' From Joseph Bentley's Day Book, May 1804. 'To Mr. Patchet, Blake Carr in Thornton. 31st Sept 1803, attending you with Act of Parliament for inclosing Thornton-common. Copy of an award of Allotment of Common alloted to Abraham Knowles. Journey to your house. Notice to fair copies to John Wright not to use a way in your land. Also a notice that two copies not to divert the water running under your covered way, from the well in his lands to the well in your lands, and to make foul the water by ducks or pigs &c. Costs 10/6'.

As in previous generations, School Green is still a part of Thornton, less rural perhaps than when only a handful of dwellings, the Grammar School and a farm or two surrounded the cross roads of the little lane to Allerton which ran down the steep Pitty Beck valley and up past Allerton Hall — built in 1777 by the Firth family, of which John Firth, whose monument is in St. James's church, Thornton, founded a bank from where he issued his own monetary drafts known as 'Firth Notes' — and the old, main Thornton Road from Bradford. A busy corner yet, fast cars disturb the tranquility now where once coaches and farm-carts swept past the ancient stone sign-post; surviving, though defaced in the war years to prevent 'Gerry' knowing his whereabouts!

Coffin End, so named from its resemblance to the shape of a funeral casket. Coffin End is a group of buildings that divide Havelock Square from the approach to the National School, and is an interesting example of the characteristic pattern that occurred in this township, particularly on the north side of Market Street. In the 19th century houses and plot shapes were made to fit the boundaries of the land, hence Coffin End. Further street alignments took little notice of the direction or intensity of landscape slopes and rights of way could also exercise an influence with public footpaths winding down into the village centre and skirting plot boundaries. In the 19th century also came the introduction of yards reached from the street by means of a covered arch. Examples of yard properties brought about by estates having houses along one or both sides are Back High Street and Ball Street.

Tram services to Thornton began in September 1882—but it was not until 1900 that finally the village was linked with Bradford! The early route, operated by steam vehicles, ran only to Four Lane Ends via Sunbridge Road, City Road and Thornton Road — conveyance further was a matter of horse and trap or 'shanks pony'. However, from Tuesday, December 18th 1900, an electric tram service was provided between Thornton centre and Four Lane Ends. Following a ceremony of inauguration, upon arrival at Thornton, the party where entertained to lunch at the Great Northern Hotel — and the Bradford Observer noted, 'In Thornton there has been some agitation in favour of the adoption of a penny fare to cover the whole journey, and a deputation of three of the leading residents of the township appointed at a Rate Payer's meeting, waited upon the Tramways Committee in the course of the opening proceedings'.

The main road to Thornton from Bradford originally ran by way of Crossley Hall and Leventhorpe Mill along the present old road, and proceeded through School Green into Market Street and thence down Kipping Lane – but following a need for safer and faster communication between village and town, in 1826 a new Turnpike Road was built under the management of Nicholas Wilson, which bypassed Market Street, and subsequently shops, the Co-operative Store and New Roadside Congregational Church sprang up on either side of the highway. The tram gave way to the trolley bus, and no longer was there a tram terminus outside the Great Northern Hotel, where a 15 minute service bumped and rattled passengers just over two miles to Four Lane Ends, where until 1902, a change of vehicles and an additional penny fare saw them safely into Bradford town centre.

Originally part of the Queensbury Society, at a meeting in Thornton's Mechanics' Institute in June of 1908, it was decided to promote an independent Co-op in the village, as the feelings of many as expressed by one, was that Queensbury was 'up in the clouds' to Thornton people. Following negotiations, the Thornton Co-operative Society opened its doors for trading on April 7th 1909. So successful was the venture, that numerous changes took place within ten years to cope with customer's demands, and the purchase of a farm up West Lane, provided stabling for transportation. In 1927, to provide further accommodation for more horses, carts and such, a fine imposing two-storey barn was built alongside the West Lane farm and exists today as Springhall Works. The late 'Twenties were halcyon days for the Co-op movement, and two further branches were opened, on Market Street and Chat Hill Road.

Headley, the principal hamlet of Thornton which consists of Upper and Lower Headley, is possibly the oldest settled area in the district, and many funeral urns of Ancient Britons have been found here. When Thornton was young, Nostell Priory had land in Headley during the 13th century, and there is an oblique reference in 13th century field-name documents to a castle or fortified site at Headley. The house itself, Headley Hall, now a farm, was erected by the Midgley family, lords of the manor in the 17th century but who were resident here long before. In the west wing is an inscription which states 'W. Midgley, 1589'. A later inscription, 'JM 1604', over the porch possibly reflects building enlargements of the period. There is much old woodwork, particularly in the upper rooms where many are panelled with oak wainscoting. The Midgley family were mentioned in two military surveys, one in the time of Henry VIII and the other in James I's days.

The fountain head of Thornton, the present Thornton Hall, hidden from view behind the ruins of the 'old bell chapel' is of 17th century date, but its origins undoubtably go back into antiquity. This was the manor house, possibly a residence of the Thornton family who held lands here in 1230. The first Hall would probably have been a timber-framed building. In 1566, Richard Tempest was described in an Inquest Post Mortem as 'of Thornton Hall in Bradford dale'. In 1608, the Burial Registers record 'Robert, son of Michael Burraye, Thornton Hall'. In 1620, it was in the possession of William Illingworth, miller. By the 18th century, in common with many of Bradford's halls, it had been divided into cottages, and in one, in 1822, lived the church clerk and sexton. A pleasing feature, is the old sundial of 1778 on an outside wall which came from the church.

Thornton Hall Farm is often thought to be Thornton Hall itself. A substantial property, it dates back to the 17th century but the present façade owes its origins to the rebuilding of the Foster family of Black Dyke Mills, Queensbury.

When I lived at Thornton it was occupied by Mr and Mrs Brown, a lovely old couple who introduced me to the delights of the garden, where much of the masonry from the old Bell Chapel of Patrick Bronte was carefully built up into an archway and ornamental feature that had gone unnoticed for many years.

Built sometime after 1850, 'Woodland Cottage' up West Lane, was erected as a mill owners residence, and in 1866, George Townend, manufacturer of Peel Bros. & Co. lived here. By 1836 however, it was the residence of Mr. William Downs, Jnr. Justice of the Peace, whose family ran nearby Thornton Mill, now Downs Coulters. Traditionally a textile centre, it was in the area of Hugill Street close by, that David Wright gave up hand-loom weaving and erected 'Old Mill' in 1826 for the purpose of spinning by 'throstle' (machines) — and this too is incorporated into the Downs Coulters complex. Wright also acted as agent for Richard Fawcett of Bradford, selling his weft and warp, on commission of 2/6 per warp, and 1/- per gross for weft, to the smaller manufacturers of Thornton. When he gave up manufacturing, he was producing three to five hundred pieces a week — a far cry from when Jonathan Wright in 1800 'shouldered down' to Bradford his four or five weekly pieces!

Another of Thornton's rural hamlets is Hoyle Ing. Of great antiquity, there is a house here dated 1588, and bearing the initials TL and EL. These possibly refer to the Leventhorp family, or of some predecessor of the Toby Lawe who had the misfortune to loose their estates and had to buy them back. Hoyle Ing is first documented in the local Court Rolls under the year 1595, when it is recorded that Tristam Bolling, of Bolling (died 1502) in his will, made over to John Tempest, son of Richard Tempest, part of a tenement called Rowle, and a house in Thornton 'newly built in ye holeyeng, of Wm. Feder'. Consisting chiefly of farmsteads, in 1704 the Land Tax Records value Hoyle Ing at £2.0.0d.

Despite many 19th century writer's description of Thornton, there were those who saw it differently. Mr. Leyland (author of **The Bronte Family**) wrote 'Thornton is beautifully situated on the northern slope of a valley, with green and fertile pastures spreading over the adjacent hills; and wooded dells with shady walks beautify and enrich the district'. Certainly this is true of the Pinchbeck Valley between Chat Hill Road upward to Thornton, and it was in the lower reaches of this valley that the ancient Corn Mill of Thornton stood — and a walk along the beck side below St. James's church still reveals traces of the mill-race which turned the great water-wheel that drove the mill-stones. Work on demolition was begun in September 1949.

Connecting Thornton with Hill Top, still an isolated hamlet of which it is recorded, that often residents fought with those from the lower village, West Lane served a number of mills, notably Upper Mill, which today is absorbed into Downs Coulters mill complex. The old cottages, middle left, have since been demolished.

Incredible as it may seem, a quiet Sunday on Market Street today would present a scene of scarcely any difference — except that electricity has replaced gas, and the lamplighter, like so many worker's in the 20th century, would be unemployed! Here is the old centre of Thornton, Field court is an 18th century building, as are those to the immediate left.

In May of 1900, the Education Committee of Thornton Co-operative Society passed a resolution 'That we recommend to the Board of Directors the desirability of providing a 'Children's' Summer Treat and Gala' – and so began an event that was for many years an outstanding feature of the village calendar. The yearly procession often consisted of six or seven hundred children, who paraded along the main streets of Thornton to the accompaniment of some noted brass band, and decorated Co-op horse, carts and wagons.

The first gala was thrown open to everyone who cared to attend, and the practise was continued. Buns and tea were provided for the children, as well as sports and prizes, in the field, adjoining the farm in West Lane. Ever in the vanguard of providing village festivities under the pretext that such events were up-lifting for the youth, in the winter month's, the Education Committee introduced a children's treat at the approach of the Christmas season. This proved to be a very attractive item, and it is recorded of the first that, 'the organisers witnessed one of the merriest and happiest collections of youngsters that it was possible to get together. There was a good entertainment and carol singing, and the coming of Father Christmas put every child into a state of wild delight'.

The actual date of Dole Mill's erection cannot be fixed with certainty, but a stone inscribed with the date 1887, could be seen over one of its entrances. This stone however, obviously related to extensions carried out in the year of Queen Victoria's Jubilee, the same year that these Warp Room employees posed for this photograph. It was built by Jonas Craven, who had as a partner Mr. Harrop. In 1876, the mill was in the ownership of the firm, Craven, Brailsford & Co. but by 1894, it had become the property of Messrs. Briggs, Priestley & Sons. Sadly, it burnt down in 1924.

Dominating Pinch Beck valley at Thornton were numerous mills, coal mines, a brewery, and gas works. And beyond which was the magnificent 20-arch viaduct. Three hundred yards long, it stood 120 feet at the valley floor and was built of local quarried stone, under the supervision of John Rowlands, of Tenby, North Wales, who is buried in the churchyard of St. James – the old Bell Chapel.

The stone trade was an important industry in Thornton, and the sandstone found in large quantities about the district was held in great esteem for general building purposes. The original quarries, many founded in the 18th century, were only small, and known locally as 'delfs' — Delf Hole being a common place-name — but by the 19th century, large commercial quarrying had been established, and tiny communities sprang up with curious names like Moscow, Egypt and World's End! A product of the large-scale quarrying (as from Egypt Quarry above), was vast amounts of 'waste' which had to be disposed of. One way was to construct huge, high walls, like the 'Walls of Jericho' opposite, and back-fill with detritus. This, a listed monument, has now gone, but a number of smaller examples remain. In the 1870s as many as thirty quarries were recorded in the Thornton Local Board district.

Walls of Jericho, Egypt.

In the Parish Registers of Thornton church, is an entry recording the death of Thomas Horsfall, who perished through an accident in this trade. 'Oct. 5th 1797. Thomas, son of Timothy Horsfall, late of West Scholes in Thornton, miner. Killed in a slate quarry upon Thornton Moor. Aged 20'. In 1876, wages were given as 'from 2s per week for boys, who began in some cases at 8-year-old, to £1 10s/£2 for adults. Barers, from 28s per week; Delvers from 35s; Hewers, 33s; and they work 50 hours per week'. — Wm. Cudworth, Round About Bradford.

Standing detached at the junction of West Lane, Kipping Lane and facing onto Market Street, the Bull's Head Inn was one of the three oldest public houses in Thornton, and was mentioned as existing in the days of Patrick Bronte. A complex building architecturally, its origins were 17th century – but whether it was firstly an alehouse only I do not know. Certainly a handsome property, such inns as this in a village were the focal point for many activities, and its position meant that following meetings a fair number would air their differences under its old oak beams.

In 1866, the Bull's Head Inn was run by Sarah Pearson, who also had charge of the Wellington Inn and the Rock & Heifer! But by 1872, it was under the ownership of Matthew Haygarth. Sadly in the late-1920s, it was reduced to a ruin soon to be demolished. Because of its position, central to Thornton, it was passed by all with business in the village, and its blank wall facing onto West Lane became the focal point for 'bill stickers'. Any notice of important event was carefully posted on its ancient walls. Thornton cinema displayed the latest films – and local Bradford football matches were advertised here.

Demolition of the Bull's Head Inn opened up the whole of Market Street, and the façade of the Black Horse Hotel was revealed. In 1866 Joshua Bennett ran it, however, its origins went back considerably earlier and in 1822 a Money Club was held at the house of Mr J. Pickles, Black Horse Inn.

From this point commenced Kipping Lane, leading into Lower Kipping Lane. 'Kipping' which gave its name to a hamlet of Thornton, is derived from the stocks which once stood hereabouts, and which can be seen preserved in the grounds of Thornton Hall. In the Middle Ages, to hold and keep fast the culprit in the stocks was termed **Kippos** in Greek and **Kippus** in Latin. The Thornton stone 'Kip' was situated in an 'ing' or meadow – thus Kip Ing was probably the name by which the site was originally known.

The majority of Kipping was developed on land owned by the Reverend James Clarke Franks and comprised an estate of artisan's dwellings which on its sale included the site for the New Road Congregational Church but not the church itself which was only begun in 1869. The estate of Upper Kipping also encompassed the Wellington Inn on Thornton Road and the Cavalry Inn off Lower Kipping Lane opened after 1872, with its dour entrance and 'domestic' exterior.

Civic Sunday, and a parade of the men of Thornton's 'A' Company Home Guard marching along Market Street. During July 1917 the scholars of Thornton Grammar School according to the School Records, 'enthusiastically supported various war efforts. Two collections of eggs, fruit and cakes have been made to St Luke's Hospital. 200 chaff bags [horses feeding bags] and 700 sandbags have been made, whilst there have been War Saving Certificates issued to the value of £330'.

As early as 1863, a company was formed to promote a rail link between Halifax and Keighley up the Thornton valley, however, it was not until 1878 that a service came to Thornton — and that, four years after the first sod was cut! The delays were due to the difficulty of the terrain, and the original scheme was finally reduced to a Bradford-Queensbury-Thornton section only. The promoters of this scheme were a group of local businessmen under the direction of Foster of Queensbury, and included Ackroyd of Halifax and John Crossley — the local carpet magnate whose mills employed several thousand people. Contractors for the line were Messrs. Benton and Woodiwiss whose experience of railway building had come the hard way when a few years earlier, they had battled against appalling weather conditions to construct the highest part of the Settle-Carlisle line. On being opened to passengers on October 14th 1878, the Bradford Observer hailed the event as an 'important epoch' in the history of Bradford-dale.

By September 1964, once proud Thornton Station, winner of the British Railways 'Best Kept Station Award' occasionally, had gone — lost to the Beeching 'Axe' — but its status as a goods yard was still secure, and the huge stone warehouse 130ft in length, 50ft high and the stone wharf 538ft in length still bustled. Thornton's main freight consisted of timber, coal and livestock transportation, and enormous pens were built to accommodate waiting animals. Interestingly, Thornton also formed the centre of a substantial 'maggot' industry, and large quantities left the station daily for angling shops around the country (bottom left). Packed in wet sawdust, in special containers with air holes, it was not uncommon for thousands to escape in summer months as they sought relief from overheating!

Thorntons maggot trade was run by Messrs. A. Bryant and Co. in Earlings Quarry, between Denholme and Bradford. Here carcasses were cut up and boiled, horses slaughtered in the 'knackers yard' and stench produced or 'effluvia' among polite circles - circles who believed that the breathing of such animal odours was beneficial to consumptives - and it was here, in 1911, that Bryant & Co. conceived the idea of inviting sufferers to inhale 'the gasses given off by sitting in the same room and at the side of troughs in which the maggots are actually breeding.' 'Patients' helped pass the time by reading and playing cards. Such was the interest, that the company drew up plans to build a sanatorium of two stories on the site - to replace the private chambers above. In this, patients would sit in comfort on the first floor and breathe through holes, the stench of breeding maggots on the level below!

INDEX